Filibuster

by Martha London

Consultant: Emma Ryan, Social Studies Educator

BEARPORT
PUBLISHING

Minneapolis, Minnesota

Credits

Cover and title page, © wellesenterprises/iStock and © Macrovector/Shutterstock; 5, © Musa Visual Media LLC/Shutterstock; 7, © Tktru/Wikimedia Commons; 9TL, © REUTERS/Alamy; 9TR, © dpa picture alliance/Alamy ; 9B, © REUTERS/Alamy; 11T, © Kevin Dietsch/Getty Images; 11B, © ZUMA Press Inc/Alamy; 13, © Sipa USA/Alamy; 14, © ART Collection/Alamy; 15, © Chronicle/Alamy; 17, © Library of Congress/Getty Images; 19T, © Everett Collection/Newscom; 19B, © Bob Daemmrich/Alamy; 21, © Drew Angerer/Getty Images; 23, © Pacific Press/Getty Images; 25T, © PeopleImages.com - Yuri A/Shutterstock; 25B, © SeventyFour Images/Alamy; 27, © Pool/Getty Images; 28T, © Al Teich/Shutterstock; 28C, © Alex Wong/Getty Images; and 28B, © Christopher Halloran/Shutterstock.

Bearport Publishing Company Product Development Team

President: Jen Jenson; Director of Product Development: Spencer Brinker; Senior Editor: Allison Juda; Editor: Charly Haley; Associate Editor: Naomi Reich; Senior Designer: Colin O'Dea; Associate Designer: Elena Klinkner; Product Development Assistant: Anita Stasson

Quote Sources

Page 28: Stacey Abrams from "The Filibuster, Explained," *BrennanCenter.org*, April 26, 2021; Barack Obama from "Obama: Filibuster Makes It 'Almost Impossible' to Govern," *The Hill*, Nov. 20, 2018; Mitch McConnell from "McConnell Defends Filibuster: 'You Don't Destroy the Senate for Fleeting Advantage,'" *Axios*, Jan. 26, 2021.

Library of Congress Cataloging-in-Publication Data

Names: London, Martha, author.
Title: Filibuster / Martha London.
Description: Minneapolis, Minnesota : Bearport Publishing Company, 2023. | Series: In the news. Need to know | Includes bibliographical references and index.
Identifiers: LCCN 2022007537 (print) | LCCN 2022007538 (ebook) | ISBN 9798885091947 (library binding) | ISBN 9798885092012 (paperback) | ISBN 9798885092081 (ebook)
Subjects: LCSH: United States. Congress. Senate--Freedom of debate--Juvenile literature. | Filibusters (Political science)--United States--Juvenile literature.
Classification: LCC JK1276 .L66 2023 (print) | LCC JK1276 (ebook) | DDC 328.73/071--dc23/eng/20220401
LC record available at https://lccn.loc.gov/2022007537
LC ebook record available at https://lccn.loc.gov/2022007538

For more information, write to Bearport Publishing, 5357 Penn Avenue South, Minneapolis, MN 55419. Printed in the United States of America.

Contents

Blocking a Vote 4

Bills Passing Through 6

Small but Mighty 10

Talking or Silent 12

A Long History 14

Useful or Not? 16

More Filibusters, More Problems . . . 20

Calls for Change 22

Here to Stay? 26

Voices in the News 28

SilverTips for Success 29

Glossary 30

Read More 31

Learn More Online 31

Index 32

About the Author 32

Blocking a Vote

Lawmakers in the U.S. **Senate** are at a standstill. Some senators are ready to vote on a new law. But others will do anything they can to stop it. They keep talking for hours. What's happening? It's a filibuster!

The longest filibuster lasted more than a day! In 1957, Senator Strom Thurmond spoke for 24 hours and 18 minutes.

Senators meet in the U.S. Capitol building.

Bills Passing Through

The Senate helps make new laws. But there is a lot that happens before something becomes a law. First, the idea for a law starts as **bill**. Senators talk about what is in it. They **debate** and change the bill until most of them can agree.

The U.S. Congress is made up of two groups that make laws. The Senate is one. The House of Representatives is the other. While the Senate allows filibusters, the House does not.

There are 100 people in the Senate.

Next, it is time to vote. But not if there is a filibuster! A senator may keep talking to block the vote on a bill.

How can this be stopped? The only way is for at least 60 percent of senators to vote that the debate is closed. This is called **cloture** (KLO-chur).

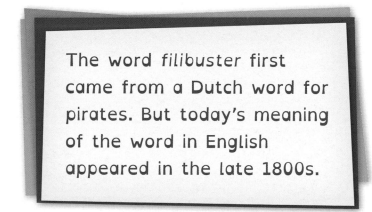

The word *filibuster* first came from a Dutch word for pirates. But today's meaning of the word in English appeared in the late 1800s.

Senators meet and vote.

Small but Mighty

Any senator can use a filibuster. But it is most common for senators in the **minority party** to do so. This group has fewer people. They often want something different than the larger **majority party**. Filibusters let senators in the smaller party stop bills they do not like.

The United States has two big **political parties**. They are the Republican Party and the Democratic Party. Most senators belong to one of these groups. Senators often vote the same way as others in their party.

Republican
Tim Scott

Democrat
Elizabeth
Warren

WWW.ELIZABETHWARREN.COM

WARREN

TEXT FIGHT TO 24477

Talking or Silent

Sometimes, a senator filibusters by talking without stopping. This is the talking filibuster.

But there is also the silent filibuster. Senators warn they will use the talking filibuster to block a vote. If enough senators say this, the bill may never even get debated.

A talking filibuster is less common because it is harder to do. The senator cannot sit, eat, or use the bathroom.

Senators may meet outside the Senate chambers to discuss votes.

A Long History

U.S. senators were not the first to use filibusters. It started long ago in ancient Rome. A Roman senator named Cato the Younger would speak for hours. He wanted to stop votes for laws he didn't like. Since then, filibusters have been used in several countries.

Some people call U.S. Vice President Aaron Burr the father of the filibuster. In 1805, he suggested changing Senate rules. Burr wanted to let senators talk for as long as they wanted.

Aaron Burr

Cato the Younger

Useful or Not?

By the early 1900s, U.S. senators decided filibusters could be useful. Those in the minority party saw it as a way to stop bills they didn't like. With filibusters, the bigger party could not always get its way.

Senators can use filibusters to say why they don't like a bill. They may suggest changes to the bill. But they can also talk about whatever they want. Some senators have read from books or songs.

Senators in 1899

17

But with the good came the bad. Filibusters have been used to stop important bills. In the 1930s and 1940s, they were used to block **civil rights** bills. In the 2010s, filibusters stopped major bills about **taxes**. Seeing these bills get blocked made some people say filibusters are harmful.

Filibusters are not always allowed. Bills about the U.S. **budget** cannot be blocked. This rule makes sure the country has the money it needs.

Senator
Strom Thurmond

Senator
Carlos Truan

More Filibusters, More Problems

Senators have used filibusters more often since the late 2000s. Because of this, people have continued to say filibusters are not helpful. They say it is bad for senators to stop votes about laws.

Since 1917, senators have used filibusters 2,000 times. More than half of those have happened since 2009.

END THE FILIBUSTER

#ENDTHEFILIBUSTER

Calls for Change

Because of the problems, many people want change. Some say the Senate should change its rules about cloture. They say fewer senators should be needed to stop filibusters. Others want to get rid of filibusters completely.

Some people believe filibusters give the minority party too much power. They say this goes against the country's first laws. These laws say the majority must be allowed to rule in the House and Senate.

WE DEMAND

1) END THE FILIBUSTER

2) PASS ALL PROVISIONS OF THE FOR THE PEOPLE ACT

3) FULLY RESTORE THE 1965 VOTING RIGHTS ACT

Some people say the Senate should change rules about which bills can be stopped. They want healthcare and voting bills to be protected from filibusters. Health laws can help people pay for doctors and medicine. Voting laws can make sure all people have a fair chance to vote.

Some senators have used filibusters against healthcare bills. They said the laws would cost too much. Others thought the bills were needed to help people.

Here to Stay?

There are senators who want to keep filibusters and others who want to get rid of them. But for a change to happen, most senators need to agree. Because of this, using filibusters may never fully go away. But how might it change in the future? Only time will tell.

Over time, senators have said different things about whether they want to get rid of filibusters. They sometimes change their minds when their party becomes the majority.

Mitch McConnell *(left)* and Chuck Schumer lead the Senate.

Voices in the News

People have many things to say about filibusters. Some of their voices can be heard in the news.

Stacey Abrams
Politician and voting rights activist

"Protection of [voting] is so [basic] that it should be exempt from the filibuster rules."

Barack Obama
Former president

"Adding the filibuster, I think, has made it almost impossible for us to effectively govern."

Mitch McConnell
Senator

"If your [bill] can't pass the Senate, you don't scrap the rules."

★ SilverTips for REVIEW

Review what you've learned. Use the text to help you.

Define key terms

bill   filibuster
cloture   Senate
debate

Check for understanding

Explain the difference between silent and talking filibusters.

Why do senators use filibusters?

What needs to happen for senators to get cloture and stop a filibuster?

Think deeper

Do you think the Senate should get rid of the filibuster? Why or why not?

★ SilverTips on TEST-TAKING

- **Make a study plan.** Ask your teacher what the test is going to cover. Then, set aside time to study a little bit every day.

- **Read all the questions carefully.** Be sure you know what is being asked.

- **Skip any questions** you don't know how to answer right away. Mark them and come back later if you have time.

Glossary

bill the idea for a law

budget money spent and earned in a certain period of time

civil rights rights that each person has to be treated fairly

cloture the closing of debate to stop filibusters in the Senate

debate to talk about the positive and negative parts of something

majority party the party that has the most members in either the House or Senate

minority party the party that has fewer members in either the House or Senate

political parties groups of people who have similar ideas and work to make laws that follow their ideas

Senate one of two groups of lawmakers in the U.S. government

taxes money that people must pay to the government to be used for services

Read More

Faust, Daniel. *The Senate (US Government: Need to Know).* Minneapolis: Bearport Publishing, 2022.

McDonnell, Julia. *How Are Laws Made? (U.S. Government Q & A!).* New York: Gareth Stevens Publishing, 2022.

Radomski, Kassandra. *So You Want to Be a U.S. Senator (Fact Finders: Being In Government).* North Mankato, MN: Capstone Press, 2020.

Learn More Online

1. Go to **www.factsurfer.com** or scan the QR code below.

2. Enter "**Filibuster**" into the search box.

3. Click on the cover of this book to see a list of websites.

Index

bill 4, 6, 8, 10, 12, 16, 18, 24, 28

Burr, Aaron 14

cloture 8, 22

debate 6, 8, 12

health 24

House of Representatives 6, 22

law 4, 6, 14, 20, 22, 24

Rome 14

Senate 4, 6–7, 14, 22, 24, 28

silent filibuster 12

talking filibuster 12

taxes 18

Thurmond, Strom 4, 19

vote 4, 8–10, 12, 14, 20, 24, 28

About the Author

Martha London is a writer and educator in Minnesota. She lives with her cat.